CONTENTS

The *Secrets* *from* FLAB *to* FAB

HOW TO BE SEXY FROM THE INSIDE OUT

DIEUNA PHILIPPE CHRISPIN

Publisher: Walton Publishing House
www.waltonpublishinghouse.com

The advice found within may not be suitable for every situation. This work is purchased with the understanding that neither the author nor the publisher is held responsible for any results. Neither author nor publisher assumes responsibility for errors, omissions, or contrary interpretations of the subject matter herein. Any perceived disparagement of an individual or organization is a misinterpretation.

Brand and product names mentioned are trademarks that belong solely to their respective owners.

Library of Congress Cataloging in-Publication Data under:
ISBN: 978-1-953993-58-8 (Paperback)

Disclaimer

Keeping physically active is key to a healthy lifestyle. If you have a medical condition, check with your doctor or physician before implementing any new exercise routines. If you do not have any health conditions, your doctor may encourage you to start regular exercise, which helps you control your weight, reduce your risk of heart disease, and strengthen your bones and muscles.

TO THE LOVES OF MY LIFE:

Jubilee, Luther II, and King, you three are my most precious reasons for being. You guys are my inspiration and have motivated me to overcome my struggles and become this healthier version of myself today. I have learned so much about myself through giving birth to you all and I am so proud to call myself your mother.

To my husband Luther, you make this journey much easier by staying in my corner and supporting me through it all without judgment.

To my role model, my mother, Camita Philippe, thank you for staying strong during my weakness.

To my sisters, Marjorie, Gerlise, Micheline, and Agathe. Thank you for believing in me and loving me no matter what.

To my brothers, Fadaél, and Dieunel, thank you for having my back.

To my super brother, Genel Philippe, who gives himself so freely to help others, especially me standing here. Words cannot express my gratitude to you. I am a product of your loving heart, and I will forever be grateful to you. There's not a time that I sit down to reflect on my life without being reminded of how you allowed God to use you to play such a big role in my life, my family, and my accomplishments.

I thank you.

To all my brothers and sisters and friends around the world, who support me on every level, I thank you! And I am grateful for every one of you.

To my coach and mentor, Dr. Sherrie Walton, thank you! Thank you for seeing through me and helping me put into words what I needed to express. Thank you.

FOREWORD

─────────────── ༄ ༄ ༄ ───────────────

Loving, loyal, and compassionate are three qualities that are infrequently found in one person. Having found those qualities in Dieuna Chrispin, makes her one-of-a-kind and a wonderful gift to this world where selfishness abounds so freely. Dieuna is an exemplary role model, and she freely gives of herself without expecting anything in return; she truly cares about the well-being of others.

This book is a result of Dieuna's love and care for others. She desires to spread the good news of hope to encourage others on the path to better health- spiritually, mentally, and physically. Dieuna has experienced the benefits of good health firsthand. A caring and giving person like herself cannot help but share such wonderful results to motivate others to achieve the same.

We have found Dieuna to be a lady who wears many hats and is always ready to wear one more when it comes to helping others. She does it with great enthusiasm, longevity, and ageless beauty. This book is designed as a practical, how-to guide to advance one's life. Gift yourself with the gift of vitality by reading and following the straightforward, experiential, and yet very effective guides in this book. Happy health!

Marjorie and Nixon Bony

GREETINGS, FUTURE SLENDER AND LOVELIER FIGURES

———— ༃༃༃ ————

First, I sincerely thank you for taking the time to pick up a copy of my book. I wrote this book with you in mind, and I am grateful to finally connect with you. I can't wait to read your testimonial on how the secrets and principles in this book helped you to set your goals to become the brand-new and admirable figure that you are.

Have you ever wondered how some people seem to stay slim? It seems like they have the secret to becoming lean and staying fit no matter their age or stage of their life. For some, it doesn't matter how many children they have, they simply seem to always bounce right back.

So, why do some people struggle while others seem to have a secret to health?

One of the greatest factors to staying slim and trim, no matter your age or stage in life, is to know your body type. This is the reason why not all diets or exercise programs work for all. It's not one-size-fits-all. Once you discover your body type, you can then find the program that is most effective and suitable for you.

As we age, our bodies naturally experience many changes. This is especially inevitable for women. However, we can overcome the effects of these changes by dismantling old habits, one by one. It requires discipline and a decision to live a healthy life.

In this book, you will find options including meal plans, exercise routines and detox options to help you discover what is best suited for you and your lifestyle goals. You must understand that what works for me may not work for you. What works for you, may not work for someone else. You must find your own rhythm. Once you do, you will achieve faster results than you thought possible.

Are you ready to say goodbye to unhealthy habits including dieting? Well, I have discovered the secrets to a healthy lifestyle, and I want to share them with you in this book. Once you apply this knowledge, you'll kick yo-yo dieting to the curb. You'll finally become the woman you knew you could be.

I must warn you that this is not another diet book. This book will help you break down mindset barriers. It will also enable you to become aware of your food choices and learn how to take control of them. Once your mind and body become on one accord, you will experience your best results. Feed your body daily with nutritious meals and exercises and live the healthiest life from the inside out.

MAY HE GRANT YOU ACCORDING TO YOUR HEART'S DESIRE AND FULFILL ALL YOUR PURPOSE. WE WILL REJOICE IN YOUR SALVATION, AND IN THE NAME OF OUR GOD WE WILL SET...

PSALM 20:4-5 NKJV

WHO AM I?

Before we begin this journey together, allow me to introduce myself to you. My name is Dieuna. I am a child of God, a wife, a mother of three, an author, personal development coach, and a business owner.

Growing up, my goals in life were simple. I wanted to be a wife and a mother, and I knew that I wanted to become a writer who inspired others to live out their potential. Any other achievement was a bonus.

Throughout my life, I have always been my biggest fan, and my number one motivator. I was also always aware of my individuality. This picture I have of myself, has kept me thriving to become and staying healthy despite the many hats I wear every day in life. I believe that God has allowed me to have these titles, however, in order to fulfill my purpose, I must strive to become my best self.

That outlook helps keep me grounded no matter what season I am experiencing in life. I also rely on self-motivation, to help me remain healthy both on the inside and outside.

My Weight Struggles

I gave birth to my first two children in 2005 and 2007. I was much younger and active, and it wasn't difficult for me to shake the weight off. Thankfully, I gave birth to them naturally without any complications. I was able to get right back on track with my health almost immediately after both of my pregnancies.

After two children, I thought I was done having kids. In fact, my first child, my daughter, was a miracle because according to my doctor, I wasn't able to naturally conceive. But not only did I conceive one child, but I also became pregnant a second time.

Today I feel beautiful after having children.

Having my son was a bonus. I believe it was God's way of showing me that through His grace, we can change our story. I wrote about these miracles in my first book, *Love Will Prevail, Only with God's Grace.* To my surprise, what man said and what my husband and I believed to be true, was a lie. God had His own plan for us.

Fast forward twelve years later and I became pregnant with my third child. This time the delivery was so different. I didn't have a natural childbirth as I did with the others. This labor resulted in a cesarean birth. Everything about this birthing experience felt different.

After giving birth to my son, I was mentally, emotionally, and physically affected. My body didn't respond as it had the first two times. It had been twelve years since my son was born, and I was much older.

In addition to dealing with the changes in my body, we were experiencing financial hardships. The stress of being broke and broken, caused me to gain more weight and become depressed. I went from being the most active and vibrant person who couldn't wait to tackle whatever the day had to offer, to not wanting to wake up in the morning. I was stressed, miserable, and frustrated with the negative emotions plaguing me.

My vibrancy for life escaped to the point where I couldn't even enjoy my loved ones. I was constantly in a blue mood zone. I stopped taking care of myself. I had gained so much weight that I was barely recognizable. I couldn't look at myself in the mirror without feeling sad and ashamed. I was ashamed to be naked in my own bedroom.

Mentally and physically, I was exhausted. When I did exercise, it didn't seem to help because of my terrible relationship with food. I was constantly craving food although I told myself that I was dieting. No matter how hard I tried, I couldn't stop eating. The more I tried to stay away from junk food, the more I craved it.

For the very first time, I felt the messy business of giving birth and the effect it had on my hormones. I used to enjoy talking about health and losing weight, but at that moment, I felt defeated. I couldn't hear those words without feeling emotionally wounded. I discovered that it's easy to talk about health when you are healthy. It's also easy to talk about weight loss when you are not overweight.

One day it turned on like a light switch and I had my wake-up call from God. I can't put into words what exactly happened, but I felt like I had received the unsolicited answer to my prayers. I finally realized the problem and I knew what I had to do to change it. I started to understand what was happening to me. I began to understand that my body had changed because it was digesting things differently, thus affecting my metabolism. I also began to realize that my mind and body were connected and that what I was feeding my body was causing mood swings.

What Changed for Me?

I had to change. I needed to prove to myself that I could do it. So, I placed an elevated level of responsibility on myself to lose weight. I started showing up for myself with the same level of commitment I had for my family. This included dragging myself out of bed to do the work on me. I started showing up for myself and taking responsibility for my health and my weight. I consequently had to shift my approach from dieting to a change of lifestyle, which made the journey easier and brought about positive results. This new discipline trickled down into every area of my life, and not just food.

One secret I learned through my journey is that losing weight surprisingly has little to do with food. It has everything to do with every area of your life. Losing weight also has to do with your mindset, whether it's a growth or a fixed mindset. That is why I encourage you not to go on a diet but go on a lifestyle journey. Was this disciplined life easy? Heck no! There were times it was the last thing I wanted to do. There were many highs and lows, and although I wanted a better outcome, my habits and my behavior didn't always support what I said I wanted to achieve.

Sometimes my thoughts were self-defeating, and my actions aligned with those thoughts. I would physically show up to the gym, but my mind would convince me that it was pointless and that I couldn't lose the weight. I allowed those negative thoughts to cause me to feel defeated and overwhelmed with a sense of failure.

There was so much about my mindset that needed to shift. I had to learn how to take responsibility for my life and my choices. I had to take my thoughts captive and use them to serve me. I had to change how I saw myself and learn to love the woman staring back at me. I decided to make a meaningful shift into positive thinking.

Our greatest power is in owning every aspect of our lives; that is, our physical, mental, emotional, spiritual, and financial parts of our lives. When we are broken in any of these areas, hurt and unhappiness become the byproduct. Accepting where we are in our lifestyle journey and making a conscious effort to make better choices for ourselves will ultimately allow us to go from "Flab to Fit." I will be sharing my journey throughout this book. My goal is to be transparent and vulnerable and offer you the exact methods I used to take back control over my life.

KEY TO SUCCESS:

TAKE ACTION: YOU CANNOT ACHIEVE ANYTHING IN LIFE WITHOUT IT. YOU MUST START. AND THE TIME IS NOW. BEFORE THE REWARD, THERE MUST BE LABOR.

DIEUNA CHRISPIN

MAKE YOUR HEALTH A PRIORITY: KICK THE WIFE AND MOTHER SYNDROME

’m going to present something that may rub you the wrong way. I often hear the excuses from married women raising a family that they don't have the time to prioritize their health. They often express that the busyness of life and the responsibilities they have do not allow them to live a healthy life.

As a wife and mother, do you have a valid excuse for not always having the time to make your health your priority? Can the busyness of the roles you wear be an excuse for you not having the time to work out? On the surface, the answer to both of those questions is YES! But if you were to delve a little deeper, you would realize that these are simply excuses, as legitimate as they may seem.

Trust me, I understand. I'm a busy wife and mother as well. Let's face it, life gets complicated after having children. We tend to put the needs of our family

first and don't always have the time to take care of ourselves. I know there are reasonable excuses for why you may not have the time to devote to your fitness. But you must make your health a priority.

There is no reason good enough for you to stay unhealthy. Being unhealthy and overweight is a choice. I am not saying this to judge you. I know what it feels like to walk around with unwanted pounds and not feel comfortable with yourself.

> **Yes, it can be frustrating when your clothes don't fit anymore.**

> **Yes, it can be difficult when you are caring for a newborn and you have a surgical birth and your body is healing simultaneously.**

> **Yes, it can be hard to find yourself again.**

Sometimes it's not as simple as eating less or working out more, especially when you are caring for your children and trying to keep your sanity. And although I empathize with you, I must reiterate that being married with children is not an excuse to live a lifestyle that does not promote healthy eating and exercise. I can tell you this because I had to apply the same tough love to turn my health around. I had to challenge myself to dedicate time to my health and fitness, and take a comprehensive approach with a focus on a long-term healthy lifestyle. I had to have hard conversations with myself.

The truth is, we do everything in our power to keep ourselves together physically when trying to find a partner, but we don't expend as much energy to keep ourselves up physically, after finding a partner. Marriage is not an outlet for letting go of our ambitious standards of physicality and appearance. After being married for over 12 years, I had to admit that marriage did bring a level of comfort with my spouse. However, being comfortable should not equate to being sloppy in our appearance. Today, after 18 years of marriage I still keep myself together.

Prioritize Self-Care

It is important to take care of yourself not only physically but also mentally, before and after marriage. This is especially important to your relationship. I believe that taking care of yourself shows a level of respect to both you and your partner. Doing so will help you feel better. When you feel better, you will be a better partner to your spouse.

Most women feel better if they take care of themselves. This is one reason I endorse physical movement. Exercise releases endorphins into the brain, which are the happy hormones. I always feel ten times better after exercising, whether walking, jogging, or running in my neighborhood, on the treadmill at the gym, or the park. Exercising is a form of indulging in self-care.

My Self-Care Regimen includes:

- ➢ Getting enough sleep.
- ➢ Starting my day with a positive mindset.
- ➢ Having a prayer life.
- ➢ Drinking a fresh glass of warm lemon water in the morning.
- ➢ Writing down what I'm grateful for.
- ➢ Spending time with my husband and children.
- ➢ Spending time with family and friends.
- ➢ Working towards my goal.
- ➢ Eating healthy meals.
- ➢ Planning my workout day.
- ➢ Taking time to write and read for at least 15 minutes.

Release Your Heavy Load

As women with so many roles, it can be a struggle for us juggle everything at once. It's time for you to release the heavy load. It's time for you to release the idea that you have to do everything yourself. Oftentimes we carry such a heavy load that if we don't do everything, we feel like terrible wives or uncaring mothers. As a result, you struggle through doing it all. At the end of the day, you are frustrated, and exhausted and your loved ones feel your anger and exasperation. Your days and nights are filled with long sheets of a to-do list that you have created. You walk around wearing them like a badge of honor around your neck. It's time to stop doing this to yourself. There are people willing to help you if you would only learn to ask. Start by teaching your partner and your children how you like things done. Assign chores to family members and take some time alone each day to breathe, think and relax. When your children are younger, this will require more of an adjustment, so give it some time. When you make a decision to put your health first, you will discover ways to implement a routine and system that works. Ask God to show you how to do it, what needs to be eliminated, and what can be delegated.

BECOME WHAT YOU WANT TO GIVE.

DIEUNA CHRISPIN

★ SECRET #1 ★

YOU MUST SET YOUR GOALS

Your New Beginning can start from today. I know you can become frustrated and discouraged if you have tried losing weight so many times and it didn't work. Don't worry, this is a new day and a new beginning. I understand that frustration. Being a wife, a mother of three, a full-time entrepreneur, and a coach, I know how hard it gets to balance life.

My advice to every woman is to set personal goals for her life. This way, you have an internal mirror to reflect and focus on what you want in the present. Be patient, and don't compare yourself to anyone else. It is not a race.

You are not a victim of your circumstances, don't allow yourself to believe that for a second. We must remind ourselves that our reasons for being inactive are mostly excuses that we have fallen in love with. You will make lifestyle changes when you plan ahead. Plan ahead to eat a well-balanced diet, instead of convenient food. Plan to exercise and do it. Make time for self-care like going for a manicure and/ or pedicure. Spend some time alone - go for a walk on the beach, or spend your time reflecting. Make these all part of your personal goals.

Make Modest Goals

Making modest changes in food quantity and quality can help you manage your caloric intake. Watch portion sizes, read food labels, and stick to real, whole foods. Even if you are trying to lose weight, you still need the right balance of calories and nutrients to sustain your body.

Define your goals, decide what you need to do to reach them, and keep your eyes on the prize. Bet on yourself. You will reach your goals with the right mindset and a positive attitude.

★ SECRET #2 ★

VISUALIZE A HEALTHIER YOU

———— ୬୧୧ ————

You may have heard the saying "performance is 90 percent mental and 10 percent physical." This is very true when it comes to attaining a healthier you. Do you know that gaining or shedding weight starts in the mind? If you don't change your thoughts and your mental state about becoming healthy, you will be in for a hard fight to lose those extra pounds.

You can be in shape physically, but if your mind isn't in line with your body due to unresolved emotional issues, your exercise plan is going to take a setback. These are mental blocks that can prevent you from pursuing certain goals in life. Most people experience some type of mental block one way or another and that's completely normal. Some of the issues that usually trigger mental blocks are pressure, anxiety, stress, the fear of trying something new, failure, or burnout. Mindfulness is an important aspect of overcoming any obstacle. Instead of focusing on what is not working, spend your energy focusing on what is working.

When it comes to physical activity and losing those few extra pounds most people tend to focus more on the physical aspect. The Mental Health Foundation has shown that what's happening in our minds influences everything we do physically.

This is why mental and physical alignment is the key to any success. You must have the right mindset while exercising and be able to have a positive frame of mind to stay motivated. Without the right mindset, your exercise can easily be overlooked by the extensive list of other things you have to do especially after a long day of work.

To shift your mental state, I want you to visualize yourself as the fit person you want to become. Once you see the "fit" you in your mind, I want you to believe that you can become that version of yourself.

In addition to visualizing, below is a list of daily activities to incorporate when you wake up every morning:

1. Be grateful for your life and your loved ones.

2. Be thankful for what you have and what you are going to receive.

3. Be thankful for where you are and where you are going.

4. Picture what you want to do and remind your brain what it's like to be healthy.

Your mind is a powerful thing. Everything you do is first manifested in the mind. That's why it's so important to visualize yourself first thing in the morning. Once you are awake, begin to visualize yourself engaged in your workout. Envision how good you feel doing it and how beneficial it is to your health. The more senses you can incorporate into your vision, the more effective the practice will be.

Visualization can even improve your strength gains. 'A study carried out by the Cleveland Clinic found that you can boost strength by up to 13% by simply envisioning lifting against resistance without physically touching a weight.

Source: https://www.verywellfit.com/

Your brain is so powerful, and its mission is to protect you. But to make greater fitness gains you must silence that little voice that tells you the weather is bad, you are too tired, or you have so many other things to do. You can silence that voice by pushing a little past what you think you can do, by visualizing achieving the goals you've set out, and by developing mental strength.

★ SECRET #3 ★

HEALTHY HABITS START IN THE MIND

A new healthy lifestyle involves a change of habits that automatically allows your mind and body to work cohesively for your overall improvement. When you become enlightened and start consuming high-quality foods that nourish your body and mind, your entire being becomes aligned during your healthy journey.

When you practice good eating habits long enough, your mind will start protecting you from unhealthy eating because you have learned how to balance food in your meals. And if you ignore your mind, because you have the power to do so, your stomach will make you pay for it with feelings of discomfort.

"Change your words to get better results."
- DIEUNA CHRISPIN

The essence of the mind and body connection shows that when you feel grounded, you make better choices about your time and what you eat. You can then be conscious about what you choose to eat rather than eat as an emotional response to a stressor. It's been said that food is something universally reached for when stress occurs, and those food choices are most likely high in fat or highly processed. Most successful people have found ways to opt out, at least mentally, from their busy schedule to check within, which increases a sense of self-awareness.

Women are remarkably busy because of the many hats they wear. You might be overwhelmed with little time to survive your busy schedule, oftentimes not having room to fit in another task. I want to remind you that this is not another thing, it's everything. Everything you are, and everything you do depends on your health. To stay on top of things and truly be present, you must first be your best. Everything starts with you because everything you are busy doing requires you. Often, we are only aware of ourselves physically in the world and may ask ourselves, *"What am I doing?"* But rarely do we ask, *"How am I feeling?"* It seems like we're constantly looking for validation in what we do instead of how we truly feel on the inside. We just keep getting busier with many tasks and no time for ourselves. Although we know that taking a five-minute breather would definitely put a smile on our face and cause us to be in a better mood, we are too wrapped up in getting our tasks done and do not spare any time to check within. The truth is, when you are not your best, it's impossible to give your best. We must take time to reboot ourselves daily to be able to give our best to whatever task we are doing. I believe in quality over quantity.

So often, we get lots of things done, but we're not giving our best because we're overwhelmed. Let us focus more on how we feel about what we get done rather than how much we got done. You might be thinking "Oh", this lady doesn't understand my situation!" Well, keep reading and let me walk you through the inside of the riveting chapters of my life and you will see how much you and I have in common. The door is open; we're sisters, and I trust that you can learn from my experience.

★ SECRET #4 ★

DON'T GO ON A DIET

———————— ༄ ༅ ༆ ————————

Many women resort to yo-yo dieting as a quick fix to their health problems. I remember dieting when I was faced with life's difficulties. It's common that in life's difficult moments like stress, fear, anger, sadness, and fatigue, we create bad eating habits. These emotional cravings encourage us to eat terribly and unhealthily, as a form of comforting us.

The reality is dieting can have a domino effect on our health. It creates a void that causes stress to the body which sometimes leads to negative emotions resulting in food binging as a way to fill the void and find comfort. This unfortunately often leads to eating excessively, which can sabotage your weight loss efforts.

We say things can either work for us or against us. A diet and new eating habits are both similar because they both make you mindful of your food intake. However, they have different effects. Dieting is an unhealthy approach to weight loss and ultimately about deprivation. When you diet, you focus on what you should not have which puts your mind into a protective mode. Whereas choosing healthy eating habits gets your mind to collaborate with you for the good of your whole being.

Research also shows that food restriction has the opposite effect. Restrictions force you into survival mode and cause your body to want to eat more. Over the long term, dieting can backfire, triggering your body's survival defenses, slowing your metabolism, and making it even harder to lose weight in the future.

In the American Psychological Association, researchers found that many people who went on diets to lose weight often regained all the weight plus more. Diets do not lead to sustained weight loss or health benefits for most people. Source: https://www.apa.org

Your mind was created to protect you, and the purpose of food is to save the body from starvation. When you tell yourself that you are going on a diet, what your mind believes is that you are going to starve your body. Therefore, your mind works against that because to your mind, starving yourself can lead to death. Even though you say you're on a diet, instead, your mind hears starvation. So, there is a war between your mind and your body.

Source: https://www.nbcnews.com/better/diet+fitness

This is the reason why when you place yourself on a diet, every food that is unhealthy to the body appears appetizing and you start craving them. Your mind is working against you to protect you. Once you start eating, you can't contain yourself.

Eating in moderation and regular exercise are the key factors to a healthy lifestyle and may lead to sustained weight loss.

★ SECRET #5 ★

FOOD HAS A PURPOSE

———— ✦ ————

Food has a purpose, and its purpose is to sustain the body. Our relationship with food is introduced to us as babies and our experience varies based on the culture we are born into. This first introduction becomes the blueprint for us either developing a healthy or unhealthy relationship with food. It determines the types of foods we consume, the amount of food, and whether we eat for our health or we're led by our taste buds.

These habits can carry into our adulthood. Fortunately, it's never too late to educate ourselves. We can learn to choose wholesome foods that will benefit our health in the long term, instead of temporary satisfaction that can adversely affect our health later.

Throughout my journey and practices, I learned that some foods simply spike our appetite and cause us to eat more than we need to.

Needs vs. Wants

In addition, there is another issue we face, and that's needs versus wants. How does that play out in your diet? Let me tell you how. Certain food choices you make are simply a want because you are hungry. You ingest those foods into your body to fulfill your hunger but unfortunately, they have no benefit to your health or your weight loss goal. These types of choices are in the category of what you want, and not necessarily what you need.

Let's take a cheese pizza and a diet coke for example. Besides temporarily filling up your empty stomach and enticing your appetite to reach out for more, how do these two choices help your health, and your weight loss goal? Whenever you choose food, you owe it to your health to evaluate how the food will help you and your body in the long run.

You may not believe it yet, but tons of food that increase your hunger after you eat them, and those foods are in the category of what you crave but shouldn't consume.

Eatthis.com suggests a list of foods that will just make you hungrier. You will find this list on page 51. The more you have, the more you crave.

Most of the time, what we want doesn't usually boost our health. If we continue to choose the foods we want, we will consequently develop bad food habits. This will cause us to have an unhealthy relationship with food instead of embracing it and using it for the nutritious purpose it serves.

Without a health goal and adequate support for your weight loss journey, you will be tempted to select foods that you want versus what you need. Many people will go for the Big Mac which will temporarily gratify their taste buds. Fewer people might choose a salad based on what their body needs. If you believe that food is the primary reason for your weight gain, I would suggest you analyze your food choices and seriously consider changing your eating habits.

What Do You Think About Healthy Foods?

You must shift any negative thoughts you have about healthy food into positive thoughts. Allow these thoughts to motivate you to be selective in your choice of food. If you believe that when you eat, the food gives your body the fuel and energy it requires to stave off hunger, as well as fight diseases, then that is exactly what the food will do in your body. You are the master of your choices; your thoughts and beliefs are simply the servants that obey your commands...good or evil.

Eating for Optimal Performance

Another problem we have when pursuing healthier goals is that we eat the wrong food, at the wrong time, for all the wrong reasons. Many women don't know how to alter what they eat to give their body what it needs. Healthy people don't just eat because they feel like eating. They carefully pick what they need to eat; they choose the foods that give their body exactly what it needs to function at maximum capacity.

> *"We become what we think about most of the time, and that's the secret."*
> - EARL NIGHTINGALE

It is imperative that you put your health above your taste buds.

Your choice of food comes down to these two aspects:

1. What you want or what you need reflects your health or your taste buds.

2. Every time we choose our food, we either nourish or deprive/harm our bodies.

It will be beneficial to choose your needs over your wants. Your health improves when you eat according to what the body requires while on the flipside, your health deteriorates if you eat according to your wants and only satisfy your taste buds.

Your body is your vehicle, and your health is your weapon to fight any obstacle in life. The quality of your life depends on the quality of your body. Being physically healthy enables you to have better overall health, including in your relationships.

Taking care of your body is paramount and I wholeheartedly encourage you to do so. I don't mean simply by what you eat and drink but also by how you use your body and allow other people to use your body. This also includes what you feed your mind, which will in turn affect your physical body dramatically. You only get one body and keeping it healthy is what will carry you through life. Don't abuse your transportation. Your life depends on it.

★ SECRET #6 ★

THE LAW OF GIVING AND RECEIVING

―――――――∽৽৶৻―――――――

"We reap what we sow."

Y ou will not receive any harvest if you don't put effort into planting the seeds. Every action you take towards your goal is going to open more opportunities to reach your goal. You cannot expect to achieve anything in life without action.

Now, figure out what you are willing to give to get your health on track. What price are you willing to pay to achieve your goal? Get busy paying that price.

There's no need for you to get scared. Now, I know most people shy away when they hear that their goals will cost them something.

> *"There is no such thing as something for nothing."*
> - NAPOLEON HILL

Goal setting without actions is simply vain wishes. Action is what will decide the price you are willing to pay to reach your goal. The price is what you are willing to deny yourself to reach your desired weight. You must be willing to give up something to gain something. Invest in yourself by getting a gym membership, hiring a personal coach, or buying self-help books.

> *"Your price is time and action."*
> – DIEUNA CHRISPIN

I know you might be thinking, *"Is that it?"* Well, you'll be surprised to know the number of people who desire results without any effort on their part. And truth be told, action requires discipline and that right there is key to achieving anything in life.

We all know that it's not easy to stay fit. You need time, energy, and money, only if you want to spend it on some gear such as sneakers, an exercise mat, or workout outfits.

Generally staying fit requires absolutely no spending at all to get started. To get the most out of your routine, you need a mix of activities during your week. You need to develop a balanced exercise plan. Planning is key to developing and maintaining an exercise routine. Make plans focusing on activities you enjoy; you're more likely to stick with them.

★ SECRET #7 ★

FROM FAT TO FAB

⁓ ා ౧ ౽ ⌐

The secret from flab to fab comes down to five things:

- ➢ Trust in God
- ➢ Proper Rest
- ➢ Sufficient Amount of Nutrients
- ➢ Exercise, and
- ➢ Healthy Eating

Most of you probably know what the first three look like, but healthy eating, what does that look like? Well, healthy eating is simply a balanced diet that offers the nutrients your body needs to function properly. Healthy eating includes a wide variety of food rich in calories such as vegetables, fresh fruits, whole grains, and proteins. Eating healthy and exercising are all about feeling great about yourself and boosting your energy. Exercise and eating healthy are two of the most important things you need to do to take care of your body.

Taking advantage of natural remedies will greatly increase your effectiveness. Let's discuss each one below.

Trust in God:

Getting healthy starts from the inside out. Being connected to God and trusting in His power will give you what you need to overcome any unhealthy habits. God is our source.

According to the new report published by Christian Medical Fellowship, those who have faith carry positive health benefits such as coping with illness, faster recovery, as well as protection from future illnesses.

https://www.christiantoday.com

Proper Rest:

Helps with hormonal balance, which keeps your heart healthy, and helps you stay at a healthy weight. It reduces stress and improves your mood. It also keeps your blood sugar consistent. A good night's sleep is a gift to the body.

Sufficient Amount of Nutrients:

Nutrients such as vitamins and minerals will help support muscles, boost your immune system, increase your health, maintain a healthy weight, and help keep your skin, teeth, and eyes healthy. It will also help the digestive system function better and improve memory and brain health. It reduces the risk of some diseases including heart disease, stroke, metabolic syndrome, diabetes, and high blood pressure.

Exercise:

Regular exercise and the consumption of a healthy diet have led me and my family's life to a host of benefits, including increased energy, happiness, and health. **By combining both exercise and healthy eating into my regimen, my energy levels have been boosted and I feel more alert, both mentally and physically.**

It also changed the way I look and feel about myself. My physical appearance has changed which is a major factor in boosting self-confidence and inspiring a satisfying life. I have been more active and involved in my children's activities. And because I have been feeling and looking better through regular exercise, my sex life has improved, I sleep better and I wake up with so much energy, ready to tackle the day. Just by regularly exercising, my food choices have improved tremendously.

Healthy Eating:

Weight management lowers your blood pressure and improves your heart health. It also helps to reduce the feeling of anxiety, improves your quality of sleep, and boosts your energy.

YOU ARE WHAT YOU EAT

My Meal Plan

When I decided to change my eating habits, I not only changed what I ate but also how much I ate and what time I ate. I planned the whole transition like my life depended on it.

The very first foods I cut from my daily intake were meat, salt, and sugar. I decided that I would eat more fish, fruits, nuts, and vegetables. I must tell you that mentally I was not ready but physically I knew I wanted to change my appearance. I had to target my mind to get my body to follow my new lifestyle.

Here is a suggested meal plan. The purpose of this meal plan is to provide the body with maximum nutrition, and minimum fat, and bring the body back into balance naturally. This plan will help normalize one's weight and maximize energy. Eating this way helped me and others I coach to lose weight. This plan can be rotated from week to week substituting different fruits and vegetables.

Breakfast

- ➢ Oatmeal – ripe banana for sweetener (cook with oatmeal)
- ➢ Soy, rice milk, or almond milk
- ➢ High-fiber, whole grain unleavened wheat toast
- ➢ Distilled / alkaline / spring or other pure water throughout the day

Mid-morning snack

- ➢ Fresh apple

Lunch

- ➢ Diversified salad (sprouts, tomatoes, parsley, leaf lettuce, romaine, cabbage, carrots, garbanzo beans. etc.) Use lemon vinaigrette dressing

Mid-afternoon snack

- ➢ Handful of nuts (your choice)

Dinner

- ➢ Whole grain spaghetti or pasta (without egg)

➢ Marinara sauce (made with tomatoes, tomato paste-look for brands without salt) - onion, garlic, mushrooms, spices, and bell peppers, which add flavor and texture. Simmer for one hour without oil)

➢ Diversified salad

Some other food choices to consider

➢ Spinach, green beans, carrots, baked fish, whole wheat bread, corn, yams, banana, orange, broccoli, brown rice, fresh strawberries / blueberries, tofu, spices and herbs, beans, lentil soup, olive oil

Remember to keep your water intake up during this time. Drink distilled / alkaline or spring water throughout the day and get as much rest as you possibly can.

You can protect your heart and lose pounds by carefully selecting your meals. Healthy foods recommended for your diet include fiber-rich fruits and vegetables such a beans, berries and whole grains, lean protein, and healthy fats like olive oil and avocado.

> *I have a seven-day meal plan that I will give you access to claim at the end of this book.*

Eating the Right Foods

The Seven Top Unhealthy Foods that Increase Your Appetite

1. **Cheese** – The high amount of fat and salt is responsible for the popular obsession with cheese.

2. **Low-fat yogurts** – Yogurt is constantly promoted as super healthy, but it truly depends on which one you choose to keep you full. The higher carbohydrate load and very low-fat content will keep you looking for more to eat.

3. **Fat-free salad dressings** – Fat-free dressings are often loaded with salt and sugar to give them flavor. After the salad is eaten, the salt and sugar make us feel unsatisfied and craving for more.

4. **Foods labeled as healthy** – We tend to overeat these types of foods. Always check the ingredient list before you buy. Stay away from foods that include trans-fat, high fructose corn syrup, artificial sweeteners, and sodium benzoate.

5. **Sugar** – Refined and processed sweeteners are unrelenting in their ability to entice you to overeat and yet, don't provide nourishment.

6. **<u>Ketchup</u>** – Any food made with high fructose corn syrup, may significantly increase your appetite.

7. **<u>Muffins</u>** – Muffins are made almost completely of sugar. This sugar is rapidly digested and absorbed, leaving your body starved for more.

Instead of repeatedly reaching out for these foods that you hunger for, which do not nourish the body, try some of the best foods that reduce overeating.

The Seven Best Foods that Combat Overeating
Source: Activebeat.com

1. **Avocados** – They are packed with fiber and heart-healthy saturated fats, which both help to suppress a hunger appetite and make you feel full.

2. **Sweet potatoes** – They are a high source of Vitamin C and Vitamin A. They contain a particular type of starch that resists digestive enzymes, so they remain in your stomach, making you feel satisfied for longer periods.

3. **Oats** – Oats contain a hunger-satiating hormone, called ghrelin. They're also extremely low on the glycemic index. Be creative with it. Mix it with almond milk, honey, cinnamon, apple, or nuts.

4. **Ginger** – Add ginger to your smoothie or tea. Ginger stimulates the body, eases the digestive process, and makes your tummy feel content.

5. **Cayenne pepper** – Add a little spice to your meals. It will boost your metabolism and keep you burning calories even when you're not moving. Studies show that adding a half teaspoon of the spice to two meals a day, for at least one month will result in three or four pounds of weight loss.

6. **Cinnamon** – This spice helps lower your blood sugar levels and curb your appetite.

7. **Apples** – Apples are a secret weapon when it comes to slowing digestion and creating that full feeling for longer periods. The ingredient in apples is called pectin, which is a type of fiber found in the cell walls of many fruits, including apples. https://www.healthline.com

GET MOVING

―――――――――― ༄࿓࿓࿓ ――――――――――

My Burning Desire

I had the burning desire to lose weight. I did not allow myself to accept any excuses. I knew I could be and feel better. I felt terribly uncomfortable within myself. So, yes! I surrendered to that burning desire. My reason for exercising and being physically active became more than just wanting to lose weight. It was and still is a way of nurturing and taking care of myself. Exercising gives me the stamina to do other things I enjoy.

Prioritize your Exercise!

I started waking up an hour earlier than usual to run and do some skipping rope before work.

The best time to exercise for me is in the morning. It makes me feel good and ready to tackle the day with energy and with a clear mind. I also feel lighter while exercising on an empty stomach, as this allows my body to utilize fat stores that already exist to fuel energy rather than food that I just ate as fuel.

I also learned that morning exercises have extra benefits. A study by the Australian Institute of Health and Welfare found that exercising first thing in the morning, followed by a healthy breakfast, boosts cognition and mood. So, give exercising in the morning a try. However, if it doesn't feel natural to you, choose another time. The key is to find what works for you.

You don't have to do too much to start seeing results, but you must stay the course and be consistent. Without consistency, you will lose track of your goals and you may find yourself right where you started, if not worse.

Exercising at any time of the day has health benefits. And for most people, the right time to exercise is more about how you feel when you are exercising and how exercise fits into your schedule. But if time is a factor, it is better to squeeze in your exercise right after you wake up by waking up 15-30 minutes earlier than usual.

Schedule exercise as you would schedule an important appointment. Block off some time for physical activity, and make sure your family is aware of your commitment. Ask for their support.

If you are not a morning person, there are some great benefits of afternoon and evening workout as well. Some people feel more ready for exercising in the afternoon than in the morning. They feel more flexible, more physically energetic, and feel stronger and faster.

Some people function better in the evening than in the morning. Evening exercise can really help you blow off some steam from the stress of your day and helps you wind down before bed.

The bottom line is this: we all know we should be doing more, but how do we keep moving when our motivation slips away, or life gets in the way? You make it a priority and refuse to allow anything to stand in your way, even if that someone is you!

My Exercise Routine

You can turn your life around, regardless of the obstacles you faced or are currently facing. Get clear. Get passionate. Take a giant step towards your goal. Get started today, you can do it.

I was so hungry to reach my desired weight, I constantly saw it in my mind. So, I started doing my research and asking questions. I begin to write my plans down as to how I was going to reach my goal. Taking it a step further, I started running 1 mile 5 days a week and doing more exercises daily.

Jump Rope

I remember sharing my struggle and my plans to change my habits to reach my goal with my darling sister Marjorie. The next thing I knew, I received a box in the mail with a skipping rope and some turmeric. I called her to thank her, and I remembered telling her that I do not know if I would be able to jump.

She responded "Sis, start small by just doing 4 sets of 50 to have a total of 200 and do it 2-3 times a week." She also told me about a natural doctor who introduced me to some natural cleansers and my eating plan. This has worked well for me throughout my journey.

Later that day, I unwrapped the skipping rope, went outside, and started jumping. I struggled and stumbled; however, I did manage to finish 20 jumps, although I was completely out of breath. I bent down with my hands on my knees sweating like crazy and feeling like my heart was going to burst out of my chest.

After a while, it dawned on me that I must push myself to reach my goal. I stood up and "spanked myself on the butt" as if I was telling myself "You can do better than this and you are going to do better than this. You will not reach your goal by being lazy, get yourself up and give me 4 sets of 50."

I picked up the jump rope again and started jumping, this time with a determination to reach 50. I did it! And I did it again three more times to reach my 200 skipping rope jumps for that day. I was so proud of my achievement. Afterward I called my sister to share the good news. We laughed at how excited I was. I looked forward to doing it again the next day.

After a few weeks, skipping rope became a competition in my house. My son Luther II first challenged me by doing the same number of jumps I was doing. I was determined to pass him every time he reached my level. Then my daughter Jubilee also started skipping. My husband joined the competition and just like that, skipping rope became a fun Chrispin family activity.

My endurance began to increase and before I knew it, I was doing about 500 jumps in the morning and 500 in the evening. I still do my workout routine to support my weight and keep my energy level up by staying active and healthy.

Benefits of Jump Rope:

Jumping rope can be a fantastic way to achieve several fitness goals including:

➢ Shedding weight.

➢ Improving cardiovascular fitness.

➢ Increasing strength and stamina.

➢ Getting a workout away from the gym.

And so much more …

Start your jump rope journey now. Look at me, now doing 1,000 jumps, 5 days a week!

Using data from a national survey representing more than 19 million US women with established cardiovascular disease, researchers say that more than half of women with the condition do not do enough physical activity.

Those numbers have grown over the last decade according to Hopkins Medicine.

Source: https://www.Hopkinsmedicine.org

These results imply that targeted educational and counseling campaigns to promote increased exercise could potentially reduce the risk of cardiovascular disease as well as associated health care costs over their lifetimes.

> *"Invest in your health to avoid having to spend on your health."*
>
> **- LUTHER KING CHRISPIN**

Exercise is not just about losing weight or building muscle. Exercise can improve your physical health, improve your physique, improve your sex life, and even add years to your life. In addition, regular exercise can have a profoundly positive impact on anxiety, and depression. It also relieves stress and helps you sleep better.

Studies show that no matter your age or fitness level, you can learn to use exercise as a powerful tool to improve your energy and get more out of life. A recent study done by Harvard T.H. Chan School of Public Health found that "running for 15 minutes a day or walking for an hour reduces the risk of major depression by 26%."

Source: https://www.health.harvard.edu

Target: Belly Fat

Helpful movements to cut belly fat

> - **Walking** - You may be surprised to see walking at the top of the list, but it can pay off big time. Burning calories is key to decreasing overall body fat percentage.

> - **Running** - This is another fantastic way to burn calories that doesn't require access to any gym.

> - **Squats** - These focus predominantly on the muscles of the lower body (glutes and quads). When performed correctly, squats can be a wonderful way to burn calories and strengthen the muscles around the stomach.

> - **Leg raises** - The bracing of this movement works the abdominal muscles, hip flexors, and obliques, which can all play a part in developing a strong and belly fat-burning core.

Daily Exercises

Before you begin the following exercise routines, I suggest that you consult with your physician. Also, invest in proper and comfortable footwear. Start slowly and pace yourself. Track your progress, which can provide you with a sense of accomplishment and encourage you to keep going.

Morning exercises:

Proposed days: Monday/Wednesday/Friday/Sunday

➢ Jogging or running for 20 minutes

Afternoon exercises:
Sunday

➢ Squats: 3 sets of 10

➢ Arm circle: 3 sets of 15 forward, 3 sets of 15 backward

Tuesday

➢ Crunches: 2 sets of 10

➢ Jumping jacks: 3 sets of 15

Thursday

➢ Butt kicks: 3 sets of 15 on each side

➢ Glute bridge: 3 sets of 15

Friday

➢ Push-ups: 2 sets of 10

➢ Dancing

Night exercises

➢ Start with 100 jump ropes

➢ Stretch

Staying active is one of the best ways to keep your body healthy and improve your overall well-being and quality of life. It will keep you physically fit and able to engage in physical activities, improve blood flow, keep your weight under control, and lower your blood pressure. It will also help keep the doctor away!

> *Refer to my YouTube fitness channel to get motivated:* **_Dieuna Chrispin_**

Workout Plan

You can start right in your living room by doing some of these exercises. These tips can help you stay active and healthy whatever your circumstances ... all for free.

Include a simple warm-up at the beginning and a cool-down at the end. The warm-up should consist of gentle exercises, such as marching in place.

Indoor workout:

- ➢ Morning stretch
- ➢ 20 toe touches, from side to side
- ➢ 50 jumping jacks
- ➢ 20 arm circles, forwards and backwards
- ➢ 15 crunches

- 8 split squats
- 10 lateral lunges

  (REPEAT 2 TIMES)

Outdoor workout:

- Walking
- Jogging
- Running

To take your fitness to the next level you might need to spend a couple of dollars buying some inexpensive accessories which will open doors to a life of physical, mental, and spiritual fitness.

- Yoga mat
- Sneakers
- Fitness gear
- Jump rope
- A gym membership

Self-care is important for a lot of reasons, particularly as it helps you to unwind and look after your physical and mental health. No matter how busy you are, always make time to switch off and do things that make you happy.

Your morning exercise statements:

Say these every morning!

➢ I support my weight loss by exercising.

➢ When I exercise, I feel good.

➢ I am becoming fitter and stronger through exercising.

➢ I love my body.

➢ I take care of my body.

➢ I visualize myself at my ideal weight.

Your Exercise Plan

Sample:

➢ **Sunday**: Cardio and abs

➢ **Monday**: Full body

➢ **Tuesday**: Leg and butt

➢ **Wednesday**: Active rest

➢ **Thursday**: Cardio and abs

➢ **Friday**: Full body

Now I want you to write down your plan

_____

_____

_____

_____

_____

_____

_____

_____

_____

_____

_____

_____

_____

_____

_____

_____

_____

_____

_____

_____

_____

"

ALL SUCCESSFUL ACHIEVEMENTS ARE THE RESULT OF A PREDETERMINED GOAL.

DIEUNA CHRISPIN

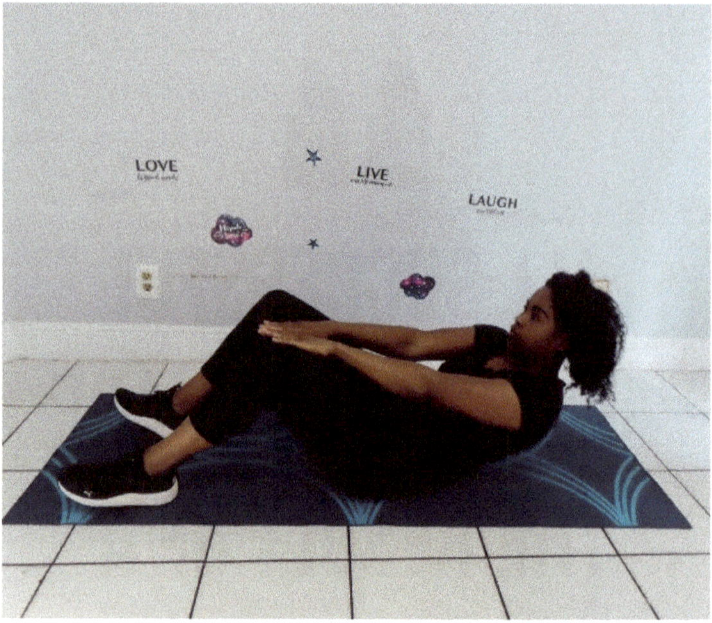
LOVE
LIVE
LAUGH

LOVE
LIVE

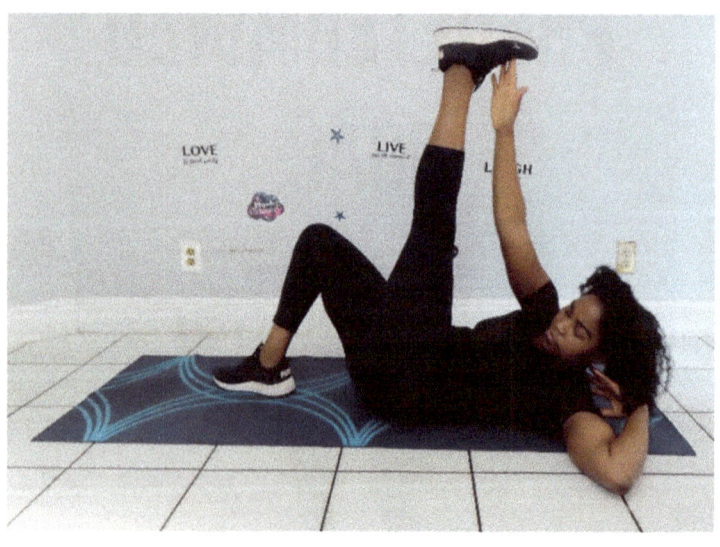

THE KEY TO SUCCESS IS THE WAY YOU SEE AND BELIEVE IN YOURSELF.

DIEUNA CHRISPIN

Personal Discipline

Discipline

S et your goals and write exactly what you want to achieve! How much time are you going to give yourself to achieve your goals?

Time setting is especially important in achieving goals because when goals are established within a timeframe prevents procrastination.

You know how much you weigh and how much of that weight you want to shed, however, the length of time it takes you to achieve those goals is just as important as setting those goals.

I know that you might be thinking, "*What if I set up a time and still do not reach my goal?*" Just because you did not meet your timeline does not mean you have failed. Not at all! Just hit the reset button and be more active and proactive the next time. But without the end in mind, you can spend the rest of your life trying to shed weight and be on a constant weight loss journey but never really get anywhere. Setting up a time to carry out your goals will push you to start working because you know there is an end.

The Push of Temptation

These 3 elements in our lives require us to live a life of significance.

1. Importance - how important is your health to you?

2. Will power - the willingness to do something about your well-being.

3. Commitments - do you have what it takes to stay the course in your health goal?

Your health is at the center of your life. Every part of your life relies on your good health. When you understand that without good health, you have nothing, you will see the importance of your health and you will do whatever it takes in your power to stay healthy and be committed to it.

Keys to Reaching Your Personal Goals

➢ Stay passionate. Do the things that you don't get paid for, but you do it anyway. When you are passionate about your goals you care for yourself and your health because you are a motivated person.

➤ Do the right thing, even when no one is watching.

➤ Believing that you can when the odds are against you.

➤ Do it to overcome your fear, not to prove anyone wrong.

Some Valuable Tips to Help you Along your Exercise Journey:

1. Knowing why you exercise is fundamental to whether you keep it up or not.

2. Do it because of the health benefits; you don't have to love it.

3. Pace yourself, don't set goals that are too big in the beginning.

4. Do it regularly and plan for it ahead of time.

5. Keep it short and sharp.

6. If one method doesn't work, try something different.

7. Stay consistent.

Mayo Clinic says that people who exercise consistently see better weight loss and fitness results in the long term. Everyone can benefit from exercise, regardless of age, sex, or physical ability. Check out https://www.mayoclinic.org/healthy-lifestyle/fitness/in-depth/exercise/art-20048389, to see the seven ways that exercise can lead to a happier, healthier you.

STAY HYDRATED

—⁓⁓—

The Importance of Drinking Water or Keeping Hydrated

Dehydration is a major problem with weight loss, and most of us do not consume enough water daily. Make sure you stay hydrated as drinking water helps to burn off fat, rather than store it within your body. Water intake helps your body function properly in terms of metabolism, mood regulation, and even energy levels. Try to drink more water throughout the day.

Science suggests that water can help with weight loss in a variety of ways. It may suppress your appetite, boost your metabolism, and make exercise easier and more efficient, all of which could contribute to results on the scale.

Source: Johns Hopkins

Daily Water Intake:

Experts often recommend people to drink eight 8-ounce glasses of water per day. This is commonly known as the "8×8" rule.

Source: Mayo Clinic

Some of the health benefits include:

- ➢ Normalizes blood pressure
- ➢ Aids in digestion
- ➢ Helps prevent constipation
- ➢ Delivers oxygen throughout the body
- ➢ Flushes body waste

CHANGE YOUR HABITS

M ost people want change but are unwilling to change their habits.

> "We get too comfortable in our uncomfortableness."
> - DIEUNA CHRISPIN

> "You must be willing to become uncomfortable to be positively comfortable."
> - DIEUNA CHRISPIN

Now, list a few of the things that you are willing to change to reach your desired weight.

_____

_____

_____

_____

_____

_____

_____

_____

_____

_____

_____

I want you to realize that you can choose to keep on or take off each pound. You are not limited to the weight you are now. If you stay like this, it's because you tolerate it. Any time you are ready to change, you are more than capable of doing so.

Please take responsibility for your weight and decide to do something about it!

If you do not take responsibility for your weight gain, it will be impossible to shed the weight simply because you tell your mind that you are not responsible for it; therefore, you will not feel obligated to shed the weight because it's not your fault.

> _"Honesty comes with responsibility."_
> - DIEUNA CHRISPIN

I strongly encourage you to take responsibility for your weight and plan how you will work on yourself to shed the weight.

Again, if you gain weight, don't be discouraged. It is so easy to gain weight for various reasons, especially with the busyness of our individual lives. I understand that circumstances sometimes happen that we do not have control over, but it is always up to us to do something about it. Keeping the weight on is not okay. If you find yourself unsatisfied or uncomfortable within your skin, you know it is time to shake it off. It is time to get comfortable with being uncomfortable.

> *"I can do all things through Christ which strengthens me."*
> PHILIPPIANS4:13 KJV

I can be that wife, the mother of my three children, and the businessperson yet, manage to stay beautiful and sexy and feel good about myself.

Look at me, being present in the moment. I still had a smile on my face even though I didn't like my weight. I knew that I was enough and that's a beautiful place to be. Especially for us women. It's important to know your worth despite your weight, age, or stage in life. Your value as a person does not change because of the many changes in your life. You are a beautiful person, and you are enough.

TO FIX WHAT YOU SEE IN THE MIRROR YOU MUST TARGET WHAT IS HAPPENING WITHIN.

———

DIEUNA CHRISPIN

SUPPLEMENTS AND DETOXING

—⁓⁓—

My Intake

Together with diet and exercise, I also boosted and enhanced my healthy lifestyle journey by taking vitamins and herbs, and increasing my water intake.

I started taking my daily vitamins and drinking more water throughout the day. I incorporated more fruits and vegetables and I slowed down on processed foods, sweets, and animal products. I fasted from food every now and then.

I also incorporated some antioxidant herbal supplements that are known for eliminating toxins from the body such as:

> **Black Walnut:** which burns excess toxins and fatty materials.

> **Chickweed:** which burns up fat and carbohydrates in your body and reduces the craving for excess food.

- ➢ **Echinacea:** purifies blood for good feeling and helps in shedding fats.

- ➢ **Papaya:** has enzymes that help to break down your food better.

- ➢ **Cascara Sagrada:** cleans the body and keeps food from building up in the colon and turning into fat.

I also detoxed through fruit and vegetable juicing, which also benefited many other women on their journey to shed weight.

Detox, My BIG Reason

I had many reasons why I wanted to shed weight, but my primary reason was that I wanted to feel good about myself, especially in my bedroom. I also wanted to be and feel healthy. Giving birth to my son by an emergency c-section had a significant impact on my mental and physical health because I was not prepared for a c-section. After the epidural (a form of anesthesia that numbs the body but still allows you to be awake), it took several hours before I could feel my body. I was unable to walk or use the bathroom on my own and I was in constant pain in the incision area for months after delivery. There were times I couldn't move from one side to the other without help. I was afraid and felt helpless because I was unable to care for my baby the way I wanted to because it hurt to sit or lay down. I involuntarily would pee on myself when I cough or sneeze. I wanted so badly to get back to normal, but I was advised not to return to my normal routine for at least eight weeks.

Emotionally, I was a wreck. I had to process my emotions about the birth because I had a c-section delivery that I had hoped to avoid. The emotional roller coaster I was on contributed to my weight gain. When I looked at myself in the mirror, I felt terrible about my size and how I felt inside.

One night, as I breastfed my baby, I looked at him and had a flashback of his birth. Immediately I started to appreciate the fact that my c-section birth resulted in a healthy and beautiful baby. A feeling of gratitude started flowing through me and I started to appreciate the fact that both my baby and I were healthy. That feeling placed an urgency within me to take care of myself so that I could better care for him. He became my inspiration to start my self-care. I also remembered what I had learned from my positive affirmation. I was taught that during hardship, there is always something to be grateful for. That day things began to change for me.

When you find your why, you have every reason to get started. So yes, I knew I needed to shed weight and I knew why I needed to do so. I also knew that my mind was my superpower and to change the way I felt and looked, I would have to stretch my mind to grow. I researched and created a list of detoxifying foods suitable for various parts of the body where the fat needed to be shed. I grabbed a piece of paper and wrote all the steps and the ingredients down. I started visualizing a slimmer version of myself with the desirable weight I longed to have. From that day, I would wake up and start the journey first in my head, and it began to manifest in my life.

Detox Juices to Help You on Your Journey

I have included some of my favorite detox drink recipes that help shed massive fat from my body. I don't want you to simply lose weight. Sometimes as women, we don't like 'losing' anything and if we do, we find every reason to get it back. So, instead of losing weight, I want you to shed it off, so you won't find it even if you look for it.

Mix the right ingredients, fruits, or vegetables with the right amount of water together.

BLEND, STRAIN, AND DRINK

(I prefer to use a blender.)

These detox drinks will help you leap out of bed in the morning. It will keep you energized throughout the day; it will clear your skin; it will put you in a better mood and it will put you on track to becoming healthy.

MORNING CLEANSING

The most powerful and yet, simple cleansing drink in my list: *8oz glass of warm lemon water*

Drink this on an empty stomach in the morning You will become amazed by what one glass of this simple remedy can do for your health and well-being.

Benefits of warm lemon water include:

1. Boost your immune defense
2. Eliminate toxic waste in your body
3. Increase your metabolism
4. Boost your energy

5. Clearer skin

6. Heart health

7. Stress relief

https://www.activebeat.com
https://www.lemonperfect.com

BELLY FAT BURNER

- ➤ ½ Pineapple
- ➤ 1 Lemon
- ➤ 1 Cucumber
- ➤ 1 piece of ginger
- ➤ 2 glasses of water

Drink 30 minutes before bedtime.

Boil the pineapple peels and the lemon peels together. Let them cool down and use the water to blend the rest of the ingredients together. Blend, strain, and enjoy.

From my table to yours.

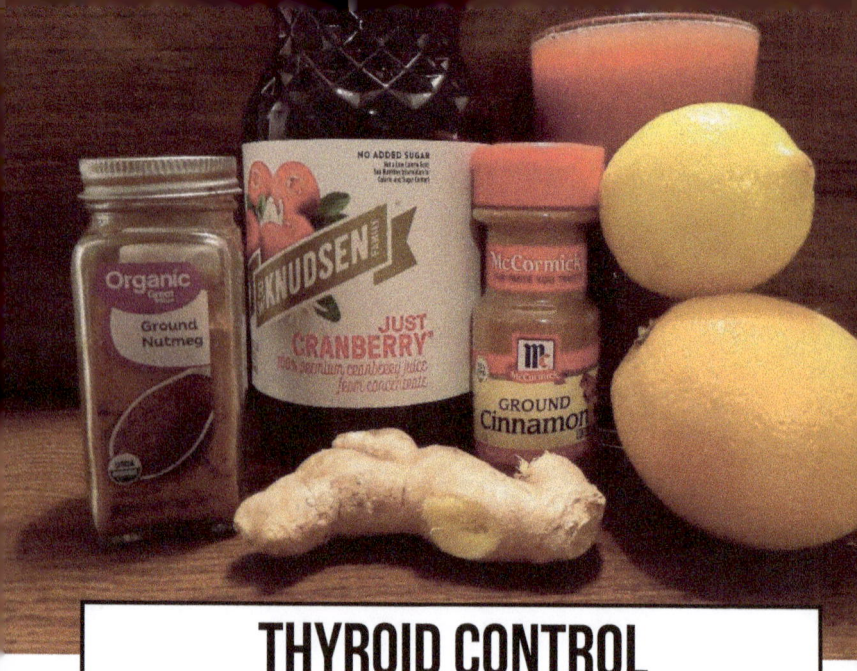

THYROID CONTROL

- ➤ 1 cup of Pure Cranberry Juice
- ➤ 1 piece of Ginger
- ➤ 1 Lemon
- ➤ 1 Orange
- ➤ 1 tsp of Ground Cinnamon
- ➤ 1 tsp of Ground Nutmeg

Here's a brief description of how these ingredients assist with your thyroid function.

- ➤ **Cranberry** has iodine which supports the thyroid function.

> **Ginger** has magnesium that helps break down inflammation.

> **Lemons & oranges** are an excellent source of vitamin C. The thyroid gland needs several vitamins and minerals, including vitamin C to keep it healthy.

> **Cinnamon & Nutmeg** are spices that offer various benefits for inflammatory disease like thyroiditis.

https://www.healthline.com

Drink twice per month

This drink is to control your thyroid and decrease your overall weight. If you do not get your thyroid under control, your journey is going to be much harder than it should. Use this whether you are looking to shed or gain weight.

Blend, strain, and enjoy

FAT BURNING JUICE

- ➢ 2 Oranges
- ➢ 2 Lemons
- ➢ 2 Pieces of Ginger
- ➢ 1 tsp of Turmeric
- ➢ 1/2 tsp of black pepper
- ➢ 3 cups of Green Tea

Drink in the afternoon

Boil two bags of green tea with the orange and lemon peel together in a pot. Let it cool down and use the water to blend the rest of the ingredients together. Blend, strain and enjoy

From my table to yours.

BELLY & ARM FAT BURNING JUICE

- ➢ ½ Pineapple
- ➢ 2 Lemons
- ➢ A handful of Ginger
- ➢ 2 Glasses of Water

Drink during the day

Boil the pineapple peels and the lemon peels together. Let them cool down and use the water to blend the ingredients together. Blend, strain and enjoy.

From my table to yours.

GET RID OF BODY FAT

- ➤ ½ Pineapple
- ➤ 1 Orange
- ➤ 1 Lemon
- ➤ Ginger
- ➤ 1 tsp of Turmeric
- ➤ ½ tsp of Black Pepper
- ➤ 2 Glasses of Water

Drink at night

Boil the pineapple, the orange, and the lemon peels together. Let them cool down and use the water to blend the rest of the ingredients together. Blend, strain and enjoy

From my table to yours.

TOTAL SKIN CLEANSING

- ➤ 5 Carrots
- ➤ 2 Lemons
- ➤ 2 Apples
- ➤ 1 Orange
- ➤ Ginger
- ➤ 2 Glasses of Water

Drink in the morning on an empty stomach

Blend all of the ingredients together.

From my table to yours.

JOURNAL &
AFFIRMATIONS

Your 'Why'

What is your **why**? When you discover your why, the journey becomes easier. You will no longer see your struggles, only your triumphs.

Jot down your **why.**

_____

_____

_____

_____

_____

_____

_____

_____

GRATITUDE AFFIRMATIONS

Once you take care of the giant that is the mind, the rest of the journey will become easier, so much so that your actions will become automatic and become part of the fabric of your new and improved life.

> ➢ I am so grateful for what God is doing in my life.
> ➢ I am grateful for my life and my family.
> ➢ I am grateful for my blessings and the many more blessings that are coming to me.
> ➢ I am thankful for my current situation, and the many opportunities coming my way.
> ➢ I am so grateful for the beauty that I see in the nature that surrounds me.
> ➢ I am grateful for my health and beauty.
> ➢ I am grateful for the ability to see the positive aspects of life.
> ➢ I am grateful for all the blessings I have in my life.
> ➢ I am grateful for the small steps I achieve towards my dream each day.
> ➢ I am thankful that with each experience I become a better version of myself.
> ➢ I am grateful for the ability to learn and expand.
> ➢ I know gratitude is a daily choice and I choose to be grateful.

Daily Fitness Affirmations

Self-talk shapes our perception of life experiences and can alter our behavior. If your self-talk is predominantly positive, positive actions will follow.

- ➢ I am fit.
- ➢ I am beautiful.
- ➢ I can visualize myself at my ideal weight.
- ➢ I deserve to be at my desirable weight.
- ➢ I enjoy eating healthy.
- ➢ I am powerful.
- ➢ I keep my body in shape by exercising.

If you have your daily fitness affirmations, I would love to hear about them. If you don't have them yet, start yours right here even if you borrow some of mine, make them your own.

My daily fitness affirmations:

1. _____

   _____

   _____

   _____

2. _____
_____
_____
_____

3. _____
_____
_____
_____

4. _____
_____
_____
_____

5. _____
_____
_____
_____

6. _____
_____
_____
_____

7. _____
_____
_____
_____

Remember: You can have as many as you want.

How Committed Are You to Your Health?

Make a list of foods which you will incorporate into your new eating habits that will help you and give you the fuel you need to keep going.

Your own meal plan:

➢ _____

➢ _____

➢ _____

➢ _____

➢ _____

➢ _____

➢ _____

➢ _____

➢ _____

➢ _____

➢ _____

Morning Eating Statements

> ➢ I am committing myself to my weight loss journey by changing my eating habits from unhealthy to healthy.

> ➢ I deserve to be at my ideal weight.

> ➢ My lifestyle and eating habits are changing my body.

> ➢ I am only eating foods that positively contribute to my health.

> ➢ I support my body with healthy food choices.

> ➢ Eating healthy makes me feel exceptionally good.

> ➢ I eat for fuel and energy to nourish my body.

I'm guessing you probably don't have your eating statements yet, and that's okay. Go ahead and write yours below.

> ➢ _____

> ➢ _____

> ➢ _____

> ➢ _____

> ➢ _____

> _____

> _____

> _____

> _____

> _____

> _____

> _____

> _____

> _____

> _____

> _____

> _____

> _____

> _____

> _____

> _____

My Before and After Picture

December 2021   **March 2022**

I lost a total of 33 pounds in 3 months during my weight loss journey.

> *If I can do it, you can do it too.*
>
> *It's possible.*

THE NOW: TRACK YOUR PROGRESS

———— ༄ঌঌ ⌐————

Remember to take pictures and measure / weigh yourself before you start your healthy lifestyle journey; this will help to track your progress as you go. Seeing a true visual of your current situation can be a magnet that pulls you towards your goal and motivates you to get to where you want to be. Likewise, your progress will encourage you to keep going because as you progress you will be able to see that it is possible and achievable.

Write down what you want to achieve and be extremely specific.

When you set specific goals, you are more likely to stick with them because these goals are unique to you, and they come from your heart and mind. Specific goals are what you want to achieve because they will make your life joyful and bring fulfillment to you and your family. Also, don't forget to surround yourself with like-minded people who will motivate you, support you, and keep you accountable on your journey.

By sharing my goals with my husband and my two older children, they were able to take part in my journey by running and exercising with me. They also held me accountable to maintain my goals and showed faith in what I had planned to accomplish by getting involved. We all need motivation in our lives.

Nevertheless, it must be your personal journey and you must hold yourself accountable for doing what you said you would do. If you mess up, admit that you messed up, and make up the ground so that you can hit that goal. When you keep to your goals, go ahead and celebrate your progress! Goal setting gives you a sense of meaning, purpose, and direction. As you move towards your target you will feel happier and stronger. As you achieve your goals you will gain strength and be able to set more goals in the future

> *"Be realistic and don't rush the process."*
> - DIEUNA CHRISPIN

It takes time to achieve positive and lasting results, so don't rush the process by looking for a quick fix. Whether you realize it or not, it took a while to get to where you are now, and it will take some time to get you to where you aspire to be. Be real with yourself about what you can carry out at this point in your life while taking into consideration your current responsibilities. Set step-by-step goals that are doable, realistic, and practical within a period. Have a time by when each goal should be completed and track your progress as you go.

If you are serious about shedding weight, you need to have a burning desire to do so and believe that you can achieve your ideal weight. This helps to keep your eyes on the prize.

Track Your Weight

Keeping a journal of your weight prior to commencing your new fitness journey, during, and after achieving your ideal weight will help you stay the course.

Your mind is at your command. Write your ideal weight on a piece of paper then every time you get ready to weigh yourself, place that piece of paper with your ideal weight over the scale glass and get excited and be grateful for achieving your ideal weight. **Have faith.**

Look at your desired weight every morning and be grateful for achieving that goal. Although it has not physically been achieved yet, it is achievable. As you begin seeing it mentally, it will soon be manifested physically. Trust me, whatever you want, picture it mentally and it will push you to work towards achieving it.

Do that for at least 90 days (about 3 months) and watch your energy boost. You will also be motivated to keep going on your weight journey. I guarantee you will start feeling better about achieving your goals. This is an act of faith.

What is faith?

> *"Now faith is the substance of things hoped for, the evidence of things not seen."*
> **HEBREWS 11:1 (KJV)**

This is a clarion call for you to start thinking and talking about what you believe could be, rather than what is.

There's no need to feel bad about your journey. It's time to try a new way of thinking about yourself and your fitness journey. No matter your weight, age, or fitness level, it's never too late to start working towards your goals. Ask your partner, your children, or a friend to exercise with you. Accomplishing even the smallest fitness goals will help improve how you think about yourself.

Create Structure for Check-Ins

Decide a day of the week for check-ins. Decide on whether you will use a bathroom scale or you will have someone take your personal measurements, and keep consistent with that. These check-ins will help keep you accountable for your progress.

I highly recommend that you follow this process, but just in case you don't have the faith to follow through, I encourage you not to weigh yourself too often as it could discourage you from continuing with your journey.

Tip:

Set a time, like once every three weeks, to weigh yourself.

"Therefore, I say to you, whatever things you ask when you pray, believe that you receive them, and you will have them."

MARK 11:24 NKJV

How to Weigh-in

First, weigh yourself, write it down and strike it through. Then, write your desired weight down and put a checkmark on it.

For example, my weight now is ~~183 pounds~~. My desirable weight is 145 pounds ☑

1 - What is your weight now?

_____ **Cross it out.**

2 - What is your ideal weight?

_____ **Check it**

CONGRATULATIONS, YOU DID IT!

‒‒‒‒‒‒‒‒‒‒‒ ꙮꙮ ‒‒‒‒‒‒‒‒‒‒‒

We've come to the end of our time together. I pray you have found the information provided helpful for you and your new healthy lifestyle. I was transparent with you about my journey, and now, I want to get to know you.

Where are you on your journey? Where do you want to go? What are your goals? I want to be a part of it. You don't have to do it alone. Too many of us are going through similar struggles, yet we feel isolated. We need each other on this journey.

If you are serious about shedding weight, contact me and I will email you an eating plan that is guaranteed to help you shed weight. As my commitment to you, I will add an electrical jump rope to your plan. I am serious about your journey.

Send me your before picture so I can cheer you on as you work towards your after picture.

Connect With Me!

- ➤ Email: **info@dieunachrispin.com**
- ➤ Website: **www.Dieunachrispin.com**
- ➤ YouTube: **Dieuna Chrispin**

Thank you for your participation and your time. You just took your first step toward a more slender and lovelier figure. And most importantly, you understand the importance of your body's needs to be wholesome and function at its best. Remember the journey will not be easy, but the results will be worth it.

Your P.D.C

(Personal Development Coach)

TESTIMONIALS

"I tried Dee's natural detox bundle and was amazed by the results after just 7 days. I dropped 7 unwanted pounds and my skin got cleared. I got so many compliments just a few days of using the detox. As a daily coffee drinker, I hesitated at first, and to my surprise, I did not miss my morning cup of joe at all. I was energetic all day. The detox is made with all-natural ingredients, and my results were nothing short of AMAZING! I referred some of my friends and they had similar results!"

- Gerlise Alexandre

"For the longest time, I struggled with my weight. I tried diets and exercises but only lost 15lbs over a long period of time. Finally, I was introduced to Dee's detoxing regimen which I applied to my diet and exercising regimen and I have lost a total of 25lbs within weeks. The jump roping was something that started off rough but over time became something as easy as walking."

- Nehemie Exume

"*Dieuna made a believer out of me that no matter how old or stage you are in life, with hard work and determination you can achieve your weight loss goal. I watch her transformation happen right before my eyes which motivated me to get into her detox and workout plans as well as referred some of my friends who needed a weight loss program to her.*"

- Micheline Philippe

"*I've always workout and used a healthy diet to keep up with my weight. However, I stopped working out for a while due to arthritis issues in my hip. I gained some weight. As I was struggling to get back into my routine, detoxifying my body was the best approach when I got introduced to Mrs. Dee's detox products. It was easier for me to start and keep up with my regimen. Furthermore, I used it as well as doing the one meal a day and was able to lose about 10 lbs. in a matter of weeks.*"

- Ketty Letang

MESSAGE FROM DR. HENRY AND RICHETTE PEARSON

———— ༺༺༻ ————

Often in life, one finds a path that leads to a better and happier life, and we believe Dieuna Chrispin has found a path that leads to a fabulous life inside out. She took on a road to a healthy lifestyle, a healthy diet regimen through natural cleansers and regular exercises to heal her body, and maintain healthiness.

In this book, Dieuna demonstrates that she understands the Law of the Eight Natural Doctors which implies to:

1. Trust in God

- ➢ to obtain peace of mind in whatever state we are in.
- ➢ strengthens the immune system.
- ➢ Relieves stress.

2. Sunshine

➢ lowers resting heart rate and blood pressure

➢ strengthens the heart

➢ increases the oxygen content of the blood

➢ decreases blood cholesterol

➢ increases white blood cells

➢ vitamin D is produced by sunlight.

3. Fresh Air

➢ helps fill the lungs with oxygen and purify the blood.

➢ Trillions of cells need air to remain healthy.

➢ Negatively charged ions in open air are good for us.

➢ Purifies, destroys, or renders inactive bacteria, viruses, and other harmful substances.

4. Exercise

➢ tones muscles and blood vessels, changing them from weak and flabby tissue to strong and firm tissue often reducing blood pressure.

➢ Strengthens the heart.

➢ Improves digestion.

➢ Increase efficiency of lungs and number of blood cells.

➢ Imparts added protection against sickness.

➢ Better sleep.

➢ Think more clearly, strengthens the will.

➢ Build endurance.

➢ Helps control body weight.

5. Proper Rest

➢ decreases muscle tension.

➢ Increases natural hormones which act as tranquilizers.

➢ Allows the body to utilize nutrients and recharge itself.

➢ Healing takes place during the early hours of the night.

6. Water

➢ cleanses tissue. Aids circulatory system.

➢ Transports nutrients and waste.

➢ Increases elimination of the mucous membrane of the intestinal tract which is an important organ of secretion.

➢ Cleanses blood, aids waste and repair. *Many diseases of mankind would not exist if people drank adequate amounts.

7. Temperance

➢ keeps everything at a safe, balanced level.

➢ Moderate use of the things that are good for us and totally abstaining from those things that are harmful.

8. Vegetarian eating plan

➢ (Fruits, nuts, grains, vegetables) aids in the health of the whole body.

➢ Live foods produce healthy blood.

➢ Organic herbs help to cleanse, build, and bring the body into balance.

We've seen firsthand how by incorporating some natural cleansers and doing regular exercises has helped Dicuna on her journey to a healthier and better quality of life, as well as her family. Therefore, as natural doctors, we recommend and encourage you to get a copy of this book and start your journey to obtain a healthier and better-quality life.

Better Health Through Nature!
God Does the Healing.

Dr. Henry and Richette Pearson

ABOUT THE AUTHOR

Dieuna Chrispin is an author, personal development coach, and entrepreneur. She is a wife, married to her best friend, Luther King Chrispin. Dieuna is a proud mother of three wonderful children. Her passion is to inspire women to get through difficult times in their lives while deepening their relationship with God with the belief that she can do all things through Christ who strengthens her.

Besides writing, and working on her dreams and goals, Dieuna loves spending time with her family. She loves adding value to others, and is passionate about helping others live a life of significance. She's also known as a John Maxwell Certified Coach, calling out all individuals to live above their circumstances.

God is the one who has enabled Dieuna to accomplish her dreams despite her adversity. God is also the one who has given her the desire to inspire others because He turned her adversity into an opportunity to grow.

This is your time!

If you do not have the time to get the detox done, I also sell them in bundles, so feel free to reach out to me for a free consultation.

Dieuna Philippe Chrispin

Here to Serve!